XTREME FISH

Eels

BY S.L. HAMILTON

A&D Xtreme
An imprint of Abdo Publishing | www.abdopublishing.com

Visit us at
www.abdopublishing.com

Published by Abdo Publishing Company, a division of ABDO, PO Box 398166, Minneapolis, MN 55439. Copyright ©2015 by Abdo Consulting Group, Inc. International copyrights reserved in all countries. No part of this book may be reproduced in any form without written permission from the publisher. A&D Xtreme™ is a trademark and logo of Abdo Publishing Company.

Printed in the United States of America, North Mankato, Minnesota.
032014
092014

Editor: John Hamilton
Graphic Design: Sue Hamilton
Cover Design: Sue Hamilton
Cover Photo: Getty Images
Interior Photos: Corbis-pgs 21 (bottom) & 26-27; Dreamstime-pg 7 (bottom); Getty Images-pgs 8-9, 10-11, 16-17, 18-19, 21 (top), 23 (inset) & 28; Glow Images-pgs 12-13, 16 (inset), 22-23 & 24 (inset); Jimmy Griffin-pg 27 (inset); National Geographic-pg 20; Thinkstock-pgs 1, 2-3, 4-5, 7 (top), 14-15, 24-25, 29 (all images on page), 30-31 & 32; U.S. Fish and Wildlife Service-pg 10 (inset); Virtual Fossil Museum-pg 6.

Websites
To learn more about Xtreme Fish, visit booklinks.abdopublishing.com. These links are routinely monitored and updated to provide the most current information available.

Library of Congress Control Number: 2014932241

Cataloging-in-Publication Data

Hamilton, S. L.
  Eels / S. L. Hamilton.
    p. cm. -- (Xtreme fish)
Includes index.
ISBN 978-1-62403-448-0
1. Eels--Juvenile literature.   2. Marine animals--Juvenile literature.   I. Title.
597/.43--dc23

                                                    2014932241

Contents

Eels 4

Species & Location 6

Habitat 8

Size 10

Shape 12

Teeth 14

Sense of Smell 16

Eyesight & Hearing 18

American Eels 20

European Eels 22

Moray Eels 24

Conger Eels 26

Fishing For Eels .28

Glossary 30

Index 32

Eels

Eels are snake-like fish, but they are not related to snakes. The largest eels may reach 13 feet (4 m) long and may weigh up to 80 pounds (36 kg). Some eels are shy, while others are very aggressive.

XTREME FACT – Eels have rows of sharp teeth. When frightened or hunting, they attack fiercely. Eels either eat their prey whole or snap off large chunks.

Species & Location

There are about 700 species of eels. They have existed for about 100 million years. Eels are generally found in warm, tropical waters of the Earth's seas and oceans. However, some live in freshwater, such as American eels, European eels, and mottled eels.

An early eel fossil found near Haqel, Lebanon. It was alive about 95 million years ago, during the Middle Cretaceous period.

Eels are found in both saltwater and freshwater. Many saltwater eels live in coral reefs (above). Freshwater eels like rocky-bottom lakes and rivers that give them places to hide (below). Many of these eels live their lives in freshwater, but travel to saltwater to reproduce. They are known as "catadromous."

Habitat

Eels like to be sheltered. They live in holes, under rocks and logs, in masses of plants, and in other protected burrows.

Three species of moray eels make their home in the same hole.

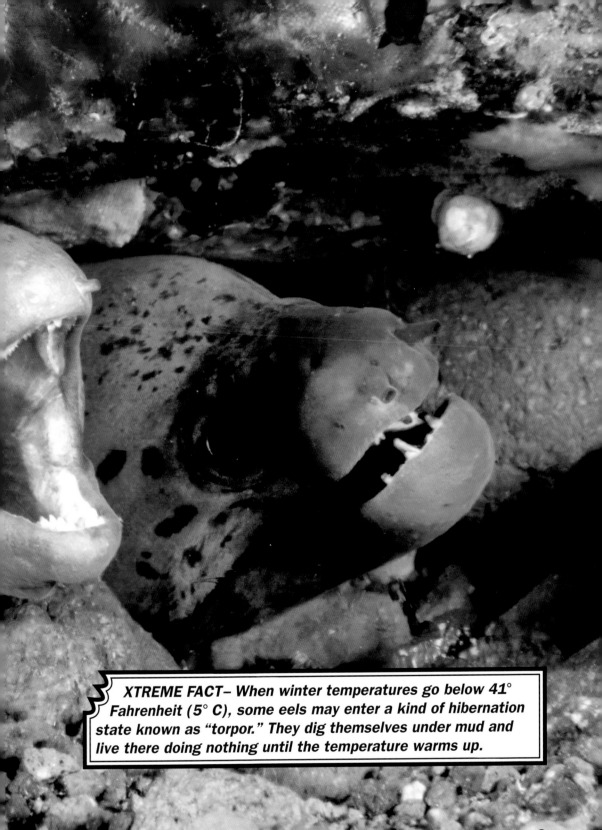

XTREME FACT– When winter temperatures go below 41°
Fahrenheit (5° C), some eels may enter a kind of hibernation
state known as "torpor." They dig themselves under mud and
live there doing nothing until the temperature warms up.

Size

Different eel species are different sizes. The average size of a freshwater eel is 2 to 4 feet (.6-1.2 m). They weigh about 16 pounds (7.3 kg). The slender giant moray is the longest eel, reaching 13 feet (4 m) in length. Its cousin, the giant moray eel, is the biggest in mass, weighing 66 pounds (30 kg) and reaching a length of 9.8 feet (3 m).

A United States Fish and Wildlife Service biologist collects an American eel from Missouri's Osage River to measure and tag it.

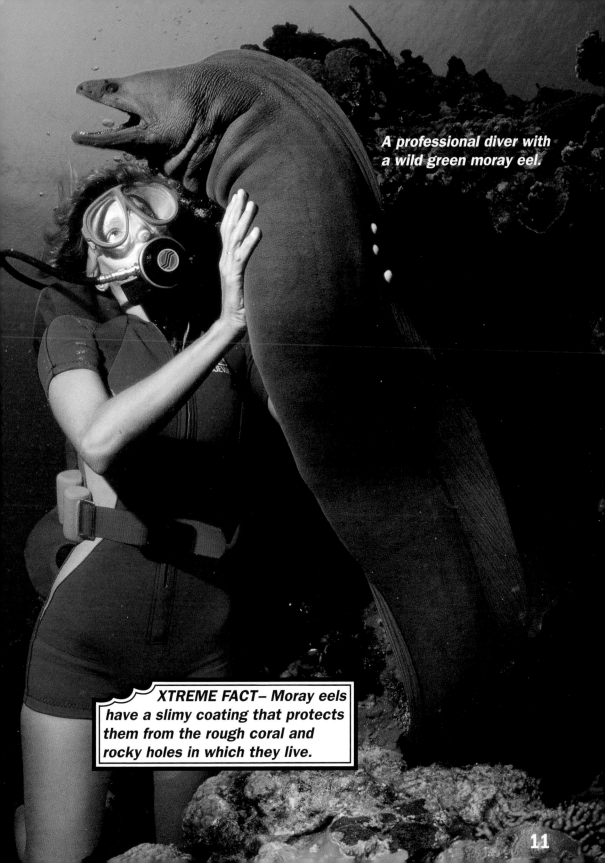

A professional diver with a wild green moray eel.

XTREME FACT– Moray eels have a slimy coating that protects them from the rough coral and rocky holes in which they live.

Shape

Eels have an "attenuated" shape. This is a long, slim body ending in a powerful tail. Their dorsal, anal, and tail fins are fused into one long fin, which begins just behind the head and runs the length of the body to the tail. This shape allows eels to wiggle into small crevices to go after prey.

XTREME FACT– Eels are one of the few species of fish that can swim backwards.

Their heads are pointed, making them very aerodynamic and fast swimmers. Their shape allows them to use little energy to propel themselves through the water. They swim in a side-to-side, wave-like movement. This is more like a snake than a fish.

Teeth

Eels have sharp teeth that point backwards. This shape snags prey and keeps it from escaping out of their mouths. Some eels have several rows of teeth. Although eel jaws are weak, their long bodies are very strong. If they can't swallow their prey whole, they use their muscular bodies to twist or spin off chunks of flesh.

XTREME FACT– Moray eels allow cleaner shrimp to enter their mouths and pick out parasites and food bits. These fish almost never eat their shrimp "dentists."

Sense of Smell

An eel pokes its nose out to smell food.

Eels prefer to hunt at night. They feel safer from predators such as birds, fish, and even larger eels that try to eat them. To hunt in the dark, eels have developed an excellent sense of smell. They use their noses to find whatever prey is available.

octopus, shrimp, crayfish, snails, frogs, toads, insects, and small birds. They will also scavenge whatever falls into the water. Eels are nature's clean-up crew.

A moray eel eats a Moorish idol fish.

XTREME FACT– It is estimated that eels find their food 98% of the time by sense of smell.

Eyesight & Hearing

Most fish have large eyes to help them see in dark, murky water. Since eels usually find their prey by using their sense of smell, they have small eyes and poor eyesight.

XTREME FACT– Sometimes an eel's poor eyesight causes it to bite swimmers or divers, mistaking humans for their food.

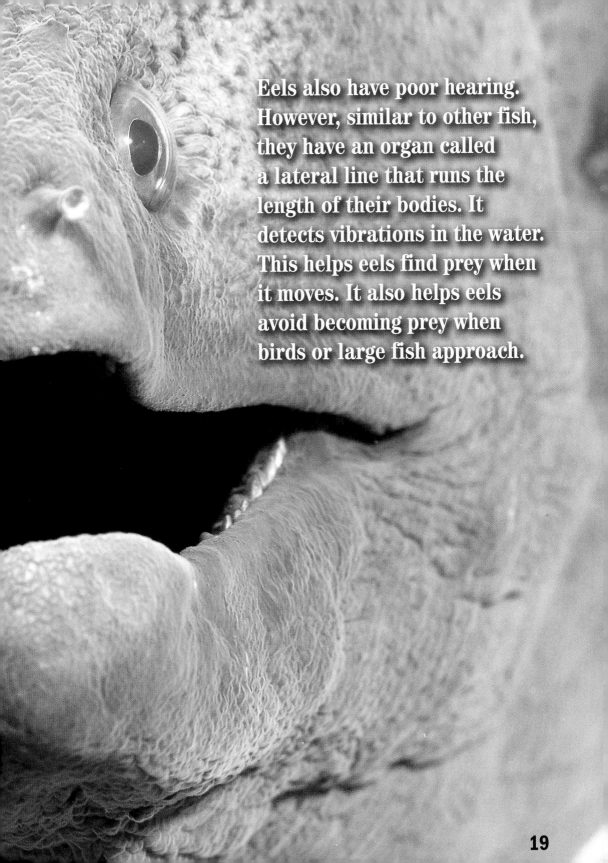

Eels also have poor hearing. However, similar to other fish, they have an organ called a lateral line that runs the length of their bodies. It detects vibrations in the water. This helps eels find prey when it moves. It also helps eels avoid becoming prey when birds or large fish approach.

American Eels

American eels are the only freshwater eels in North America. They are catadromous. They live in freshwater, but swim to saltwater to breed. They begin and end their lives in the Sargasso Sea in the Atlantic Ocean. When first born, they are see-through larvae. They grow into their eel shape, remaining transparent. They are known as glass eels.

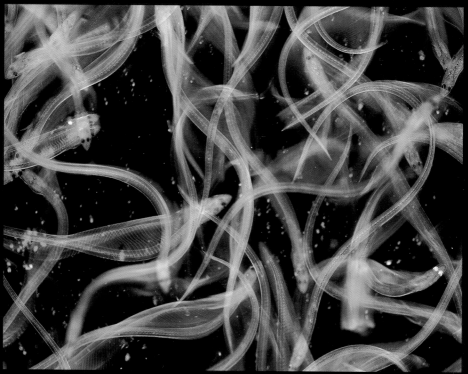

Ocean currents bring the glass eels to the eastern coastline of North America. Once there, they travel up rivers to continue their lives.

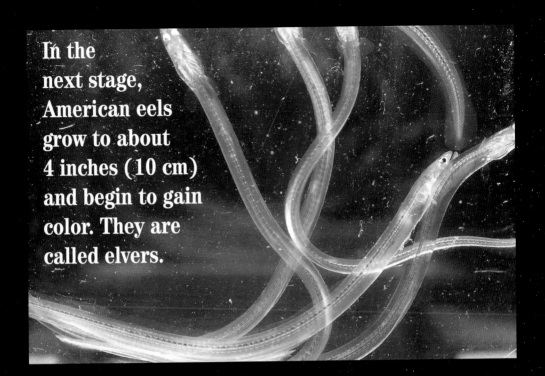

In the next stage, American eels grow to about 4 inches (10 cm.) and begin to gain color. They are called elvers.

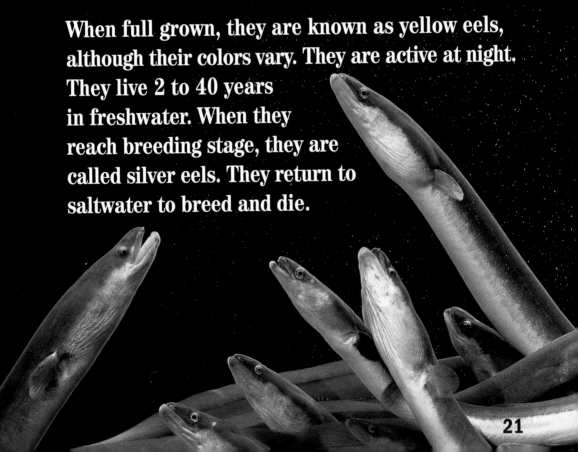

When full grown, they are known as yellow eels, although their colors vary. They are active at night. They live 2 to 40 years in freshwater. When they reach breeding stage, they are called silver eels. They return to saltwater to breed and die.

European Eels

European eels are found in European rivers and streams that drain into the Atlantic Ocean. Although genetically different from American eels, they are close relatives. European eels also begin and end their lives in the Sargasso Sea. They are also catadromous. They live their lives in freshwater, but breed and die in saltwater. Their various stages of life are the same as American eels.

XTREME FACT– Overfishing, parasites, pollution, and dams blocking their way to the ocean have caused a steep drop in European eel populations since 1980. They are listed as "critically endangered." Plans are in place to help the species.

In 1964, fishermen could haul in huge numbers of European eels.

Moray Eels

Moray eels live in warm, tropical oceans. They stay hidden in rocky crevices and coral reefs, coming out to grab their prey of fish, squid, cuttlefish, and crabs. Morays have "pharyngeal jaws." This is a second set of jaws inside their throat. This second set is launched into their mouth when they grab their prey. This draws the prey into their wide mouth. Their long front teeth tear off chunks of their prey.

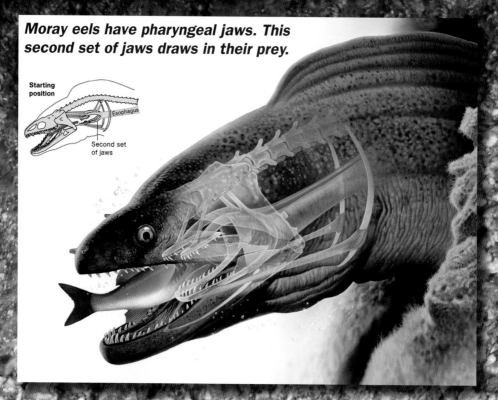

Moray eels have pharyngeal jaws. This second set of jaws draws in their prey.

Starting position

Esophagus

Second set of jaws

XTREME FACT– Morays use their long bodies to tie themselves in knots and gain leverage when tearing into their prey.

Conger Eels

Conger eels grow to the longest average length of any eel, about 10 feet (3 m). They live in the North Atlantic Ocean on rocky coasts from Iceland to North Africa and the Mediterranean Sea. Conger eels grow to great sizes by eating octopus, crab, lobster, and other fish.

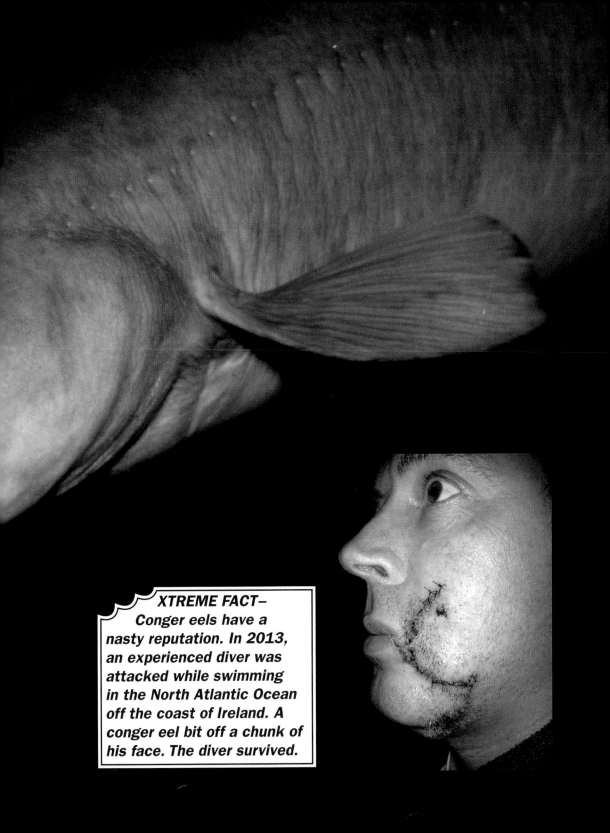

XTREME FACT–
Conger eels have a nasty reputation. In 2013, an experienced diver was attacked while swimming in the North Atlantic Ocean off the coast of Ireland. A conger eel bit off a chunk of his face. The diver survived.

Fishing for Eels

People fish for and eat all types of eels. Anglers bait their hooks with pieces of meat to catch eels.

XTREME FACT– European eel populations are so low, only a few licenses are issued each year to legally fish for these endangered species.

People also fish for eels with nets and traps.

Eels are sold alive in fish markets. They are eaten in sushi rolls. Smoked eels are also sold.

Glossary

AERODYNAMIC

Something that has a shape that reduces the drag, or resistance, of air or water moving across its surface. Fish with aerodynamic shapes can go faster because they don't have to push as hard to move through the water.

AGGRESSIVE

Likely to attack with, or without, a reason to do so.

BIOLOGIST

A person who studies living things.

CARNIVORE

A creature that eats meat in order to survive.

CORAL REEF

An underwater ridge made up of coral and other living matter. Coral reefs are home to many fish, plants, and other marine life.

CRUSTACEANS

An animal with a hard shell and many jointed legs. Shrimp, crabs, lobsters, and crayfish are crustaceans.

DORSAL FIN

The fin that is located on the top of a fish's back. On a shark, for example, the dorsal fin is the one that sticks out of the water when the shark is swimming near the surface.

FRESHWATER

Water sources with little amounts of salt in them, such as lakes and rivers. Saltwater, such as water in oceans and seas, has a higher salt content.

GENETICS

Related to the genes. The building of a living thing based on the characteristics it inherits from its mother and father.

LATERAL LINE

A visible line that runs along the sides of fish. The lateral line helps fish detect movement in the water. The sensing organ helps fish to find prey and helps them avoid becoming prey.

MIDDLE CRETACEOUS PERIOD

About 89 to 127 million years ago. A time when dinosaurs roamed the Earth.

Index

A
American eel 6, 10, 20, 21, 22
anal fin 12
Atlantic Ocean 20, 22, 26, 27

B
biologist 10

C
catadromous 7, 20, 22
cleaner shrimp 15
conger eel 26, 27
coral reef 7, 24

D
dorsal fin 12

E
Earth 6
elvers 21
European eel 6, 22, 23, 28

F
freshwater 6, 7, 10, 20, 21, 22

G
giant moray eel 10
glass eel 20
green moray eel 11

H
Haqel, Lebanon 6

I
Iceland 26
Ireland 27

L
lateral line 19
Lebanon 6

M
Mediterranean Sea 26
Middle Cretaceous period 6
Missouri 10
Moorish idol fish 17
moray eel 8, 10, 11, 15, 17, 24, 25
mottled eel 6

N
North Africa 26
North America 20

O
Osage River 10

P
pharyngeal jaw 24

S
saltwater 7, 20, 21, 22
Sargasso Sea 20, 22
silver eels 21
slender giant moray eel 10

T
tail fin 12
torpor 9

U
United States 10
United States Fish and Wildlife Service 10

Y
yellow eels 21